My Formative Years:
One to Eighty-One

By

Stephen Gary

Table of Contents

Introduction

I went to kindergarten twice. The first time, I wanted to marry my teacher until she hoisted me from the circle of my peers by the seat of my pants. She had instructed us to sit silently before nap time, but I was continuing to chatter. She sneaked up behind me, lifted me above the others, and flew me across the room to the Corner of Bad Behavior. There, I pretended not to cry while my classmates slept. Sadly, this was not the last time I was wounded by a woman I loved.

My subsequent career improved my ability to follow instructions. I was an attorney with a federal agency responsible for international energy and national security. I had a top-secret clearance, and knowing how to keep quiet was critical.

Then, I retired and needed something else to do.

My first morning in retirement I was reviewing newspaper ads for "Volunteers Wanted" when, suddenly, the sidewalk before my house erupted with raucous kids. It was 8:45, and the school across the street was opening. Until then I had been at work at the time and never saw them arrive. Now, I was amazed. Laughing and shouting at each other, they were full of life and joy. I wanted what they had.

I asked the principal if she could use a volunteer, and the next day, I was in kindergarten for the second time--as an assistant teacher.

The kids loved me, and I loved them. I taught the afternoon shift but usually arrived early to help out on the playground--that is, to play with them. I held the end of a jump rope or retrieved a ball from the area they were not supposed to enter. Then, they settled down at the front of the room to await my official arrival. They practically screamed a greeting: "Hello, Mr. G.!!" I never had a welcome like that as a lawyer.

They were full of surprises. A boy would be speaking in the most grown-up way, using words and expressions obviously plagiarized from adults in his life but making perfect sense. Then, in mid-sentence, the young scholar would humbly ask me to tie his shoelace. He was still a child.

Observing the children brought back memories of my own childhood, which led to these essays. They begin with my first formative years--my life as a toddler--then move on to college and beyond. In the last essay, I am in a different kind of formative period: I am married. I am still working on that book.

1.
Matinees

As a toddler, I sat in front of the radio for hours. I was listening to voices. I did not understand words, but was fascinated by the way they sounded. From differences in modulation, rhythm, and pitch, I conjured a face for every voice. I knew what each person looked like.

Every weekday morning, after Dad left for work, Mom cleared the dishes and did some housework. She always stopped promptly at 11 and turned on the radio. Like millions of others, she tuned in to Arthur Godfrey, the most popular program host on network radio. He chatted in a folksy manner with a variety of guests. Again, I comprehended nothing but was enamored of his mellifluous, welcoming voice.

Years later, he had a similar program on television, where I saw him for the first time. I was dismayed: he looked nothing like he was supposed to. Even after months of seeing the actual person, it was my version of him that was real.

So far, voices seemed to be random, rising from individuals without a pattern. That changed when I heard my first radio drama. It was a genre that has received more ridicule than respect, the lowly soap opera.

I was introduced to it by a woman named Catherine.

She came to our house a half day each week to do laundry. When she arrived, she turned on our small bookshelf radio and did not turn it off until she left. As she stood ironing, she listened to one soap opera after another. We became friends, and I listened with her.

I emptied my shoebox full of cowboys on the floor near her ironing board. I sat there and made up Western scenarios for them. Catherine contributed to the stories between one sudsy episode and the next. Based on my limited knowledge of the Old West, my first thought might be to make my horsemen a gang of outlaws. She always saw more possibilities. They could also be a posse of lawmen.

Soap opera plots were complex and the language arcane, but they were dramas, and had the effect of transforming voices into characters. In addition to faces, I was now creating personalities.

 At first, there was little difference between male and female characters, but I noticed a change while listening to one of the classics, "Our gal Sunday." This program was always introduced by a well-spoken baritone as "the story that asks the question, 'Can this girl from a mining town in the West find happiness as the wife of a wealthy and titled Englishman?'" I never learned the answer, but I began to understand the question.

Miss Sunday was the first character I visualized as pretty. There had been other females, but she was the first I perceived as feminine.

Soap operas were opening my eyes to the world of romance. What better place to learn? That was what the shows were about. They also taught me poetry. The first poems I heard were commercials – the soap in the soap operas. Ivory Soap set the tone. It was "99 and 44-100% pure," a rhyme that bypassed rational thought and made straight for the viscera. Like all great poetry, it appealed to a deeper sensibility. No one knew what it meant, but everyone remembered it, and it sold lots of soap.

Mom listened to the radio, too. Aside from Mr. Godfrey, she and Dad had favorite evening programs. Her true passion, however, was the silver screen. She went to the movies two or three times each week. She could not find enough babysitters for that many theatrical excursions, so she simply took me with her.

In the year I was born, 1942, film studios were producing hundreds of films a year. At the rate Mom and I were going, I would see a high percentage of them before starting kindergarten.

Unlike radio, films left little to the imagination. Mine was focused on how to escape from the theater. I considered crawling under the next row of seats to reach the exit and then finding a policeman to take me home, but I concluded I would get stuck or be caught and be even worse off.

Mercifully, I often fell asleep--not surprising for a child who would have been taking naps at home.

Ennui reached its peak in the "kissing scene." When I begged Mom to take me home, her response was, "It's almost over," but it never was. It went on forever. If two people had to suspend normal conversation to do it, couldn't they at least speed it up?"

I could tolerate musicals with Fred Astaire. In one of his movies, he danced up one wall in a room, continued upside down across the ceiling, and fancy-stepped his way back down the opposite wall. I suspected the use of tricks but was impressed.

I also liked the watery films of Esther Williams, though they too may have stretched the truth. When Mom and Dad tried teaching me to swim, all the water near home in Baltimore was murky; you couldn't see a thing. But she swam in water that, unrealistically, was crystal clear. I could see all of her, and I made sure that I did because I had decided to learn how to swim by copying her movements. I noted the reach of her arms and, especially, the hypnotic opening and closing of her long, silky smooth legs.

They affected me as Fred Astaire's did not. In fact, I spent more time attentively observing her than I did any other actor. I guess I really wanted to learn.

Most other musicals either bored or annoyed me. If there was too much talking, they bored me; if the people talking suddenly burst into song, they annoyed me. That did not happen in real life, but it happened all the time in musicals. When it did, I wanted to scream, "Stop, please stop! No one really does that!"

I was a stickler for reality. All through a movie, I would ask my mother, "Is this true? Did this really happen?" Since I would not stop until I got an answer, she devised a universal, automatic response: "Yes, dear, it's all true; it really happened." For one particular movie, the response gave me nightmares.

I saw "Kiss of Death" with Mom when it was released in 1947. I was five years old. It featured a vicious murder scene. A sadistic killer, terrorizing an elderly invalid, ripped electrical wiring from a wall and, with studied brutality, tied her to her wheelchair. He then steered the chair to the edge of a long staircase and, laughing maniacally, gave it a shove. I could not take my eyes off the chair, tumbling end over end to the landing below, where it lay concealing the victim. Not seeing the lifeless body left the full horror to my imagination.

I was terrified. Tugging desperately on my mother's sleeve, I cried, "Mommy, Mommy, is this true? Did this really happen?" She never glanced my way, eyes on the screen, contentedly munching popcorn; she simply muttered the standard response, "Yes, dear, all true." She did not notice that this time, I was not asking out of idle curiosity but from a state of abject terror. The answer that normally reassured me caused me to wake up crying in the night for weeks.

"Kiss of Death" was a classic "Film Noir," or "black film"-- characterized by dim lighting, dark themes, and violence. The films were popular and inexpensive to make, and the studios produced a steady stream. Since Mom and I were seeing nearly everything they made, we saw lots of Film Noir. This was simply the scariest.

Why would she take a young child to such a movie? Mom was more concerned with the lives of the actors than the characters they played. She was an avid reader of Hollywood fan magazines. They brimmed with details about who was married to whom, when they got divorced, and when they remarried. She tried to educate me, but I did not pay attention. They were her friends, not mine.

She selected movies not for their content but based on who was starring in them. "Kiss of Death" starred Kirk Douglas and Victor Mature, two of her favorites. That is why we were there.

Occasionally, we saw a first-rate film. In 1949, when I was seven years old, everyone was excited about MGM's tenth-year revival of "The Wizard of Oz." One of the first to be filmed in Technicolor, many thought it was the best movie ever made.

It's reopening in Baltimore got the treatment of a brand-new film, premiering at one of the grand movie palaces downtown. Originally built at great expense by the major studios to showcase only their own best and finest, they were now the favored venue for launching any costly production, regardless of its source. Lavishly promoted there, a film would later work its way to less expensive neighborhood theaters. Parents did not want to wait for this one; progeny in hand, they rushed directly downtown to Baltimore's grandest, the Hippodrome Theater.

The day Mom took me was cold and rainy. We took a cab. When the windows steamed up, the driver ran the heat and defroster full blast. The car got hot and stuffy, and the whoosh-whoosh of windshield wipers was hypnotic. By the time we reached the Hippodrome, I was barely awake.

It was magnificent, reminding me of grand ballrooms from Mom's 19th-century costume musicals. High above, behind gleaming brass rails, soared parallel tiers of balconies. The orchestral seating was enormous, row upon row of plush, maroon velvet chairs, softly cushioned, with leg room to spare. Uniformed ushers escorted patrons to them individually with a flashlight and impressive pomp.

Awestruck by the theater, I was drowsy from the cab ride and, except for the cartoon, bored by the preliminary features, which included a newsreel. I was confused when the movie began. Half asleep, I thought at first it was another newsreel because it was in black and white rather than Technicolor.

It was no accident. The film's creators had introduced a young girl named Dorothy, who lived on a farm in Kansas. Black-and-white emphasized the harshness of the environment. Soon after, a tornado lifted her house to the skies, with her and her little dog Toto still in it.

Then, after 17 minutes, the film exploded into stunning Technicolor. She had been transported to an entirely different world, Munchkin Land, causing her famously to observe to Toto, "I've a feeling we're not in Kansas anymore." But I still was. I fell asleep in monochrome Kansas and never made it to Munchkin Land.

In fact, I did not wake up until the movie was nearly over. I woke for the last 3 minutes, back in monochrome Kansas. There, we learned that Munchkin Land had all been a dream from a bump on the head. When she returned to her senses in black and white, I was there waiting.

In effect, while everyone else saw an imaginative, full-length color spectacle, I experienced a 20-minute, monochrome depiction of grim farm life in Kansas. It wasn't fair.

When, at dinner that evening, Dad asked how I liked the movie, I sheepishly replied that the theater was beautiful. I was ashamed to admit I had slept through such a momentous event.

Later in 1949, however, I experienced cinematic history first hand, and of far greater personal importance than the "Wizard." The brand new Crest Movie Theater opened its doors in my neighborhood. Its gleaming Art Deco-style marquee rose directly across the street from my home.

The advent of the Crest had special significance for Mom. Since she had never learned to drive and there had been no theater nearby, going to a movie required advance planning. She had to phone for a taxi and allow enough time for it to pick us up and drive us there. With the new theater on our doorstep, Mom could dart to a movie spontaneously. I began to hear, "Hey, Stevie, let's go to the Crest. We have five minutes before the next show." In two minutes we were seated there, a box of popcorn in my lap as compensation. Only then, often, did we learn what movie we had come to see. Mom had memorized the stars and the starting times; nothing else mattered.

There were also two huge benefits for me. First, because we could walk to the Crest, even if Mom insisted I go with her, I no longer had to be stuffed into a cab to go somewhere I didn't want to go to see something I didn't want to see. The tyranny of the taxi was no more.

Second, my neighborhood had scores of kids more or less the same age. With such a large potential audience right next door, the Crest management shrewdly developed a Saturday morning program for kids, a major improvement over the kind of films my mother had been dragging me to.

Each Saturday at 11 a.m., we mobbed the box office, clamored for a 16-cent ticket, and raced for the best seat. The program began with a plethora of animated cartoons, shown in rapid succession, from Mickey Mouse to Mighty Mouse. It was thrilling to have so many cartoon characters in one place at one time, and we were an enthusiastic audience, laughing uproariously at the antics of our favorites, but we could also be impatient. If there was the least delay in moving to the next feature we did not hide our displeasure. At first, we squirmed in our seats, complaining and whining among ourselves. The next stage was more ominous. We booed and catcalled for action, our cries getting louder the longer the screen remained blank. Finally, discontent reaching a crescendo, we launched a barrage of popcorn boxes. The beam of light from the projector cast shadows of their trajectories onto the vacant screen, giving the appearance of a frenzied flock of crows mobbing and pecking an enemy. The effect was dramatic and usually produced what we were waiting for: the weekly installment of Flash Gordon, Pioneer of Outer Space.

 This serial went on forever. Each Saturday's episode closed with the hero about to meet certain doom, but the next week always opened with a disclosure of the secret that had kept him alive. It was classic bait and switch, but it kept us coming back, and we loved it. After years of Saturdays, no one recalls seeing a conclusion. I suspect the producers continued filming until the actors got too old for space travel and then simply stopped without bothering to produce a final episode.

Finally came the feature attraction, such as "Ant Men from Mars." If it was part of a double feature--two full-length movies in a row-- the second was on a related theme, like "Return of the Martian Ant-Men." On double-feature days, we could be there until dinner time.

I don't know how many years we went to the Saturday show, and I can't remember whether the Crest stopped putting it on before we outgrew it or vice versa. Eventually, we all grew up and moved away.

I recently drove by the old neighborhood and was amazed to see the Crest still standing. Closer inspection disclosed that only the marquee had survived intact. It bore a bronze plaque designating it a historic landmark. The rest of the theater, apparently, lacked historical significance. It had been converted into an inspection station for the Department of Motor Vehicles.

Behind the marquee itself was a glass-enclosed display case. I recalled it overflowing with candies. Now, along with a few antique Snickers Bars and Tootsie Rolls, it showcased a photo of the old interior. Row upon row of seats faced a solid red curtain. I recalled what a thrill it was to see the curtain open dramatically and reveal the screen. Soon, the MGM Lion would roar, or the Paramount Mountain would rise above the clouds. Each studio had its own iconic image and unique, soul-stirring fanfare. What an experience!

Oddly enough, these reveries led me back to radio. I recalled how its shows also opened dramatically, with a theme song or slogan.

There was, however, a fundamental difference. Movies had become so technically advanced they left nothing to the imagination. If you asked patrons about a movie they had just seen, you would likely hear a similar description from each. If you showed them a photo of one of the actors, they would probably all recognize him.

Old-time radio, on the other hand, had invited the imagination to create its own reality. I recalled how I had given Arthur Godfrey a face of my invention and refused to accept his own as real. I never compared notes with my friend Catherine, but I suspect our visions of the heroine of "Our Girl Sunday" were as different as could be.

Full of such musings, at home that evening, I tuned in to a local FM station that played classic radio shows. I listened to a couple and found myself once more creating faces from voices. I was pleased to rediscover the power of imagination. It had always been there; I had simply stopped paying attention.

2.
Men in Bloom

When I was four years old, Mom, Dad, and I moved from my grandparents' home in downtown Baltimore to a home of our own. It was in a new housing development on the outskirts of town. The land it was on had been farmland since colonial times when it grew tobacco. Later, it produced corn and soybeans. Now, it was sprouting houses.

Our homes were modestly priced for new families like mine. There were lots of kids born during the War when the birth rate soared. Nationwide, parents needed someplace to put us all, and builders responded with inexpensive, basic homes. Ours was typical.

We had no ball fields or playgrounds. Including them in the project would have raised the price of homes too high for many first-time buyers. We simply played in the streets. There was not much traffic. However, other areas were off-limits. These were remnant patches of fields and pastures where the original farmhouses had been left standing. Years of poor harvests had left them in disrepair and had induced their occupants to sell the surrounding acreage. They received more from developers for the land than it was worth for agriculture, but they insisted on retaining title to their homes and remaining in them. The result was an odd amalgam of old and new.

Across the street from my home was a weather-worn, dilapidated structure a hundred years old. Our parents viewed its occupants as different and warned us not to go there. As kids, we found the differences appealing and visited them often. They bred rabbits, which they allowed us to play with, and raised chickens. Each dawn, from my 20th-century bedroom, I heard roosters crow from 19th-century chicken coops.

Several years later, in a matter of days, the house was gone. Someone had purchased it and an adjacent pasture to build a shopping center with a host of small shops. Like ducklings in a row, they trailed behind the gleaming, Art Deco-style structure at the entrance, the brand-new Crest Movie Theater. Dominating it all was the splendid marquee, with a façade of brilliant white bordered by bands of chrome.

It was directly across the street, where the chicken coops had been. I no longer heard roosters, but the marquee was so close I could read every word from my bedroom window.

One Saturday night, after the theater had gone dark, the marquee burst into light again. Startled out of bed, I rushed to the window. All week, the title of the current movie, "Robin Hood," had been spelled out in bold, black letters against the glowing white façade. Now, some letters were missing.

Peering through the glare, I noticed a crouching, jump-suited workman. Beside him on the ground lay a ten-foot pole, and nearby, the letters R, O, and B. I realized what was happening. The Crest changed movies weekly, and he was taking apart the old title to spell out the new.

He attempted to pick up the pole, but it was unwieldy and fell from his hands. Apparently, he had dropped it after removing three letters. Now, he crossed himself and, firmly planting his feet, raised the pole once more. I watched him reshuffle the alphabet for hours.

From then on, I observed the weekly transformation whenever I could. Balance was always a challenge. Sometimes the pole went flying, sometimes the man.

Through all the changes, however, two words remained the same. Bigger and bolder than the rest, they were fixed in place: "COOL INSIDE." The reason was simple. To Baltimoreans in summer, the fact that the building was air-conditioned was more important than what was playing.

Each July, a blanket of soggy air enveloped the city. We called it "humidity" and debated whether it or its cousin, high heat, caused greater suffering. There was no doubt in my mind: humidity won hands down. Heat discouraged physical activity, but humidity caused me to ask myself, "Do I really have to breathe? Is it worth the effort?"

Electric fans were no solution. They merely recirculated the problem. Only air conditioning could extract moisture from the sodden air, but no one had central air conditioning at home. Fortunately, I had it across the street.

Only a few steps away, the Crest was also inexpensive. Most patrons went to the movies at night when the price of a ticket was $1.50. To fill empty daytime seats, the Crest's management had reduced the afternoon price to fifty cents. Besides, since no one cleared the house between shows, I could stay as long as I liked. On especially oppressive days, I might view the main feature two or three times. I got to see all the nuances.

In the summer, I had no school and dropped in often to cool off. The quality of the film mattered less than the outside temperature. The hotter the day, the lower my standards. I didn't care what time the movie began. If I entered in the middle, I merely stayed through the end and saw the beginning later. Seeing a movie backward that way was a problem for murder mysteries: I learned who committed the crime before I knew what the crime was, let alone the identity of the suspects. That made for less suspense, but I stayed cool.

Anyhow, box office times were approximate. A movie scheduled for 2 p.m. might not begin for another hour. It all depended on the "Selected Short Subjects" that always preceded it. These cinematic odds and ends varied greatly in type, length, and quality. Because they were not listed on a playbill, the audience never knew what was coming. How they got to be "selected" was anyone's guess. They could be real duds.

For me, the worst were the travelogs. What did I care about Bermuda when I got around on a bicycle? I wasn't going anywhere.

Then came a day in July when the temperature and humidity both reached 100—100 degrees and 100 percent. Together, they left me no choice: I would have to spend hours at the Crest simply to breathe. Yet that was the day for a rarity: a short subject of quality, a film that changed my life.

Produced by Walt Disney Studios, "The Secret World of Plants" was not animated like "Snow White" and other Disney classics but was a groundbreaking nature documentary. It used innovative time-lapse photography to reveal the development of plants from seed to blossom.

Each frame of film was shot at a rate much slower than normal, giving the appearance of the action taking place faster when projected onto the screen. The film showed a seedling sweet pea vine climbing towards the sun. In life, its progress was too slow to be seen, but the film compressed two months of growth into two minutes on the screen.

The plant waved its growing tip randomly in the air until, by chance, it touched a nearby sapling. Then, it sent out finger-like tendrils, which grasped a branch and curled around it, providing a secure position from which to repeat the process and climb higher. The plant seemed human, like an infant reaching for a hand, its tiny fingers grasping and curling around an adult thumb.

The film portrayed nature in a whole new light. Plants were no longer passive objects but active participants in their growth.

It concluded with a parade of flowers coming into full bloom, one after another. First was a hibiscus, still in bud. Through seams in the green cover, I noticed a hint of red. The seams gradually widened, then suddenly split open, revealing crumpled petals, still tightly folded upon themselves like a lady's collapsed fan. Then the fan opened explosively. Blazing scarlet petals unfurled full-size, their protruding yellow stamens seeming to blare like trumpets. The blossom filled the screen.

Next was a lily, then a rose, then a dozen others in rapid succession, each in its own unique manner. The effect was overpowering.

When the final crescendo concluded, I ran to the exit. I wanted to buy seeds to replicate the miracles I had seen. In my excitement I forgot to open the door slowly, as I always did, but pushed it open in one swift movement. I paid the price. It was like opening the door to a hot oven and putting my head in. After two hours of coolness, the summer heat almost knocked me down. Regaining my balance, I ran the rest of the way.

The Crest Shopping Center had all kinds of family-owned shops. Only minutes from my home, I could find anything from bakery buns to buzz saws—the latter at my favorite, Greenburg and Sons Hardware.

Weaving through its crowded aisles, I loved the challenge of guessing the identity and purpose of the jumbled tools and gadgets. If stumped, I simply asked a Greenberg. One was always nearby.

Outside the store in summer, with a seasonal assortment of rakes and hoes, was a Ferry-Morse seed display. It contained row upon row of packets, with pictures of blossoms on the front and instructions on how to grow them on the back. I had passed the rack for weeks without a second glance. Now, I thoroughly combed the envelopes for just the right seeds. I wanted a vining plant like the sweet pea in the film, and found one with larger and bolder flowers--the morning glory.

To observe the growth of roots, I wanted a transparent container, but all I could find was Mom's Pyrex glass measuring cup. She relied on it for cooking, and I was afraid she would not let me use it. Too excited to take the risk, I "borrowed" it. Pangs of decency made me return it the next day, but I was less than candid: "Look, Mom, I found the measuring cup you misplaced." Obsession was eroding my morals.

While flowers were totally new to me, I had been dabbling in filmmaking for a year. My mother's younger brother, Uncle Danny, was a professional wedding photographer. For my birthday, he gave me a movie camera and taught me how to use it. He might have regretted it when he saw what I was filming.

I practiced on relatives at family gatherings, capturing them in candid moments I thought were amusing. I would make a film at a wedding, develop and edit it, and then show it at the next social event. I did not intend to embarrass anyone, but I sometimes misjudged sensibilities. A cousin and an aunt asked me not to bring my camera again. An uncle warned me not to return at all.

I had resolved to avoid this minefield and find safer subject matter when I discovered the Disney film. The timing was perfect. Flowers were more attractive than my relatives, and they did not complain.

Over the next several weeks, I learned the meaning of patience. Time-lapse cinematography was not difficult; it was simply boring. With the camera fixed to a tripod and aimed at the subject, I had to remember to press the shutter release at the same time every day to record a day's growth one frame at a time. I did this daily for two months. It was tedious, but the film was a success—at least in the living room.

My silver screen was a bed sheet hung from a curtain rod. On it, the morning glory seed sprang to life. In minutes, it sent out networks of roots, stems, and leaves and developed scores of buds. Its petals unfurled slowly at first, then burst forth, like the flowers in the Disney film. I had trouble thinking of a title and later regretted the one I chose, "Life of a Morning Glory," but it appeared so briefly in the speeded-up credits it was barely legible.

My living room critics, Mom and Dad, gave me rave reviews, no doubt pleased that I was no longer offending relatives. I accepted their gift of funds for two sequels, "The Blooming of a Lily" and "The Daring Daffodil." I was better at filming than naming.

Having observed and filmed test subjects, I excavated a plot in the backyard for sustained gardening. I ordered plants from mail-order catalogs, whose lush photographs lured me to exotic species. They rapidly died. The mortality rate improved greatly when I switched to familiar species grown in my area.

I learned which plants did well locally by asking local gardeners. If I passed a yard with an appealing bloom, I stopped to ask what it was. The resident was usually so pleased I had noticed that she gave me a plant or a cutting.

That person was always a woman. No males were in the garden, and none answered the door. In fact, I knew of no male gardeners at all. This got me worrying: what if my interest in posies was so unusual, so unmasculine, that my friends would disapprove? What if they ostracized me for being a sissy?

When I was five, a little neighbor named Ducky Doolittle invited me to a tea party. I had a crush on her and had even tried to kiss her once, but she had squirmed away. Now I was on good behavior, but after an hour with her and her dollies, I couldn't wait to leave. It was a long time before I played with girls again.

My best friend Bobbie, older and wiser, was six at the time. He said it was a good thing I had left; I might have turned into a sissy.

Now, years later, my older friends were whispering about "queers"—something like sissies, I guessed, but worse. I didn't know what they were and whether growing flowers would make me seem like one. I simply kept quiet about it.

Of course, I was jumping to conclusions. In those days, generally, men went to work, and women stayed home. When I knocked on the door to admire a plant, the absence of men did not mean they did not cultivate flowers—only that they were not home. For all I knew, the plant I was inquiring about had been planted by a male.

I told myself this, but I could not stop worrying. There was too much at stake. My friends were my family. We practically lived together. Each of our homes shared a common wall with the house on either side—a wall too thin for secrets. We spent all day at school together, then played ball in the street we lived on. The layout of our infield depended on where neighbors had parked their cars. First base was the rear tire of a Chevy; across the street, twelve feet away, the bumper of a Ford was third.

Second base and home plate were lined up along the median stripe of white paint. Each was a flattened, empty box of Wheaties, "Breakfast of Champions," the choice of our cowboy and outer space heroes. A stone kept the box from being swept away by passing cars.

We never lost anyone. The street was small enough for drivers and players to see each other in time, and sentries at either end kept watch. When they shouted, "CAR COMING!" we cleared the field, suspended play, and resumed it again when safe, seemingly in one fluid motion. We had it down to an art.

We could not afford a real baseball or the gloves and bats it would have required. Our game was punch ball. We used a small rubber ball, the Pennsylvania Pinky, available for pennies at Woolworth's. It was ideal. With houses so near, a harder ball would have broken windows. The Pinky bounced off the glass and remained in play.

The street was too narrow a field to have foul territory. All balls were fair. That got us in trouble with Mr. Kilgore.

He was a taciturn, middle-aged bulldog who lived with his wife in a house two removed from mine. They were childless and kept to themselves. The houses and lots in our neighborhood were identical except for his. He had paid for an extra-large lawn, which was impeccably groomed and bordered by beds of glamorous flowers.

We considered him the neighborhood ogre. If our punch ball landed on his property, he habitually scowled and muttered what we assumed were epithets, though no one got close enough to hear. We were too afraid. With remarkable alacrity for one his age, he pounced on our ball and kept it. He must have had the largest collection of punch balls in Maryland.

I had forgotten about him. He was a male gardener, but he did not count. He was not a regular person.

Within months of launching my career in cinema, I developed a fascination with butterflies. The progression was natural. Entranced with blossoms, I could not help but notice their glamorous visitors.

As it happened, the centerpiece of Mr. Kilgore's lawn was a six-foot tall "butterfly bush." Aptly named, it resembled lilac, but its scent was even more intoxicating. It attracted the largest, most conspicuous varieties—swallowtails and Monarchs. They could not stay away, and neither could I.

I wanted to collect and preserve them, and despite my fear of Mr. Kilgore, I was willing to take my chances.

I launched a sneak attack early one morning, hoping he would be asleep. I crawled through the grass on my belly, like Army commandos from the movies. They used their elbows for support and cradled their rifle in the crook of their arms. That was how I held Dad's long-handled minnow net.

Dad and I had used it to catch minnows for bait when we went fishing. It had worked fine for that, but it was proving useless for catching butterflies. Afraid I'd be spotted if I rose, I swept the net through the air as best I could from my knees, but capturing butterflies on the wing proved surprisingly difficult. I failed to catch even one.

I next tried a more direct approach: I focused on butterflies perched on blossoms engaged in feeding. Preoccupation with sipping nectar, I reasoned, would keep them still long enough for me to ease the net over them. That had to be easier than catching them in flight. This, too, failed and disturbed the bush. When I realized I was doing harm, frustration gave way to remorse, and I stopped.

Turning to crawl back, I was horrified to see Mr. Kilgore in a downstairs window, red-faced and glowering. He was getting dressed, and not taking his time about it. He flung his snap-on suspenders over his shoulders and reached down for his shoes. My time was near.

I had expected him to be angry. After all, we all knew how mean and bitter he was. But I saw things differently now. The punch balls and my net were harming things of beauty, which he had been nurturing for years. He did not have to be ill-tempered to react the way he did--only human. Now that I shared his love for flowers, I understood: I would have felt the same way.

Even so, he had murder in his eyes, and I did not want to die so young.

He stormed out of his front door and stomped deliberately toward me, a bull preparing to charge. I desperately wanted to run. Instead, I rose from the lawn, tossed aside the net, and looked straight into his angry red eyes. I had suddenly decided to grow up.

With only twenty yards between us, I chose my words carefully:

"I am sorry, Mr. Kilgore. I love your flowers so much I lost my head. Please let me buy you a new butterfly bush."

He stopped in his tracks. Brow furrowed with doubt, he fixed me with an intent, quizzical gaze. I did not move an inch. His face grew less contorted, but his upper lip ticked nervously--the beginning of a snarl?

I rested my case: "I love your flowers. They are beautiful."

Miraculously, he smiled. To my knowledge, in the annals of the neighborhood, this was the first time such an expression had crossed his face. In fairness, though, it was likely the first time anyone had spoken to him, let alone paid him a compliment.

He thanked me and asked if I would like to come back tomorrow for a tour. An enemy had become a friend.

I now had a fellow male gardener, and a tough one at that. No one could call the killer of punch balls a sissy.

He proved even more macho than I had imagined. The next day, as we stood chatting in his kitchen, he reached into a drawer to show me a plant catalog. Lifting a corner, he inadvertently revealed a revolver. Now that I had seen it, he asked if I would like a closer look and handed it over. It looked like a standard police firearm. As far as I knew, no one else in our neighborhood had a gun of any kind. When I asked how he happened to have it, he explained he was a security guard for the B&O railroad, which ran along the edge of our neighborhood. I was certain no one else knew his secret, but I was the one who needed it most for my own self-esteem. A gardener with a gun was no sissy, and neither was I.

I soon realized something that helped me grow further. Mr. Kilgore was not a man because he had a gun but because he had the courage to pursue his calling--the courage to be himself. I was beginning to feel that way about myself, and I liked the change. Instead of brooding about what might be wrong with me, I would try being grateful for what was right.

Decades later, my former punch ball comrades and I were meeting for a weekly reunion breakfast at a Baltimore deli. For the past ten years, one of them had been sending emails to those of us still alive and, by mistake, some who were not. He advised every one of where we would be meeting, a different restaurant every week.

I was late finding out about it. Most still lived there, but I had moved forty miles away and had lost touch. After receiving the first email, I rushed there before we lost another member.

In Lenny's Deli, the conversation naturally ran towards the old days, and someone mentioned punchball. For the first time, I told them the tale of reconciliation with our old nemesis.

They all listened intently, but one of my oldest and closest friends, Alan, seemed particularly engaged. He had a wry sense of humor and a mischievous twinkle in his eye, but he seemed serious now, genuinely moved. He eased his head nearer to mine, and I expected him to comment on how fine it was that a shared passion had brought Mr. Kilgore and me together. Seemingly breathless with emotion, he whispered in my ear: "I have something important to ask you."

"Sure, Alan, go ahead."

"Did he return our punch balls?"

3.
The Pond

My father was a lawyer in Baltimore. Every July, he and a few friends chartered a boat for a day of fishing on Chesapeake Bay. All were self-made men. The eldest and wealthiest was Mr. Teril. Dad was the youngest, and his income the smallest, but you'd never guess he belonged at all from the way he dressed. A product of the Great Depression, he was saving up for the next one by skimping on clothes.

Dad bought his suits from bargain bins at discount stores. Despite Mom's admonitions, he refused to stop wearing them when they developed cigar holes. He kept a cigar clenched in his teeth. It was a feature of his face, but he rarely smoked it. He would forget the cigar was lit until hot glowing ash dropped to his lap. He'd feel a burn and brush it aside, revealing a new hole. If I saw no holes in the pants he was wearing, I knew he had just bought them.

 In that regard, he loved to show me his new purchases: "Would you believe I got this shirt for three dollars?"

"That much?" I'd reply.

The men were sons of poor Jewish immigrants. I once asked Dad, "How poor was your family?"

"We didn't have an indoor toilet," he replied. "I had seven siblings. We took turns waiting outside on cold nights."

"That was poor," I agreed.

As they rose in the world, all but Dad moved to successively larger homes. With his penchant for saving, he preferred money in the bank; we never bought another home after our first. We simply stayed there.

Mr. Teril was different. He had retired and wanted no more of city life. He lived on a sprawling estate in adjacent Baltimore County—near but worlds apart.

The county was home to Maryland's social elite, who engaged in fox hunts and the breeding of thoroughbred racehorses. He never expected his neighbors to pay him a call and was not disappointed. He did not care. As he explained to Dad and me: "They inherited their money. What do they know of life?"

Besides, he had not moved there to mingle with high society or raise horses; after a lifetime of hard work, he simply wanted a spacious, peaceful place to rest. He had found it.

Dad and I loved to visit. We enjoyed his broad, rolling meadows and the abundance of towering shade trees. Summer days were always cooler there.

One day, the subject of their next fishing trip came up. Dad said it was too bad the chartered boat left Annapolis at dawn. Since it took 45 minutes to drive there, they had to leave home when it was still dark. Mr. Teril slyly replied that he didn't have to travel at all; he had fish on his estate.

Dad thought he was joking: "Where are you hiding them, in your well?"

"Come with me." He walked us a few yards to a higher point, one arm around my father's neck, the other on my shoulder. Pointing far into the distance, he asked, "Do you see that woods down there, by the property line?"

Squinting, I replied for both, "No, we don't. We can't see that far." It was true. The estate was vast.

"Well, take my word for it. There's a woods, and there's a pond in it."

Dad realized he was serious: "I didn't know you had a pond."

"Neither did I, and I almost forgot until you mentioned fishing. I don't like having to wake up early, either."

"When did you discover it?"

One day, about five years ago, two guys from the county showed up on my porch. I thought maybe I owed taxes or something, but they tell me they're here to discuss my pond."

"'What pond? I don't have a pond.'"

"So this guy pulls a map from his pocket. He unfolds it, and it's huge, with all kinds of lines and details on it."

'"See this green shading here? That's your woods down there."'

"He points to where I tried to show you. I didn't even know I had any woods."

"'Okay," I say, 'If you say so.'"

"'You see this blue dot inside the green? That's your pond.'"

"'Well, how about that. I had no idea.'"

'"Yes. Well, we're here to make you an offer."'

'"You want to buy it?"'

'"No, no. The county has a mosquito-control program. We'll stock a private pond with bass and sunfish to feed on the larvae. It's free. You just have to allow anyone to fish there who asks. Can we do it?"'

"I thought a minute. I don't like mosquitoes. 'Sure, as long as it's free. Go ahead.'"

"So the next day, a crew shows up with a tank truck. They go into the woods to run a hose to the water. When they come out, their clothes are all ripped, and they're bleeding."

"'What happened to you guys?'"

"It's a jungle in there. Thorns and stuff tore us up. Don't ever go in there!"

"I never did. I never wanted to. I forgot all about it."

Dad seemed fascinated, and I thought I knew why.

"Has anyone asked to fish there?"

"Are you kidding? Who would have known about it? I didn't."

When I saw the expression on Dad's face, I was certain we both had the same idea. We subscribed to "Field and Stream" magazine for the articles on fishing. Now and then, it reported the discovery of an isolated pond that had never been fished. The fish it contained were huge, and I had never seen a hook.

Fish who had been caught were wary when they saw another line. Ones who had not were fearless, storming a lure or bait with abandon. A pond with fish like that was an angler's dream. Could Mr. Teril's be one of these pristine marvels? We thought so.

In addition, Mr. Teril's fish has been growing undisturbed for five years. They must be huge.

When an issue of the magazine had an isolated pond story, there was an eye-catching painting on the cover. It showed a fish that, from below a lily pad, had lunged so hard at a surface plug that his momentum had taken him two feet in the air. Having hooked himself on the lure, he was furiously wagging his head to shake it off, dancing across the surface on his tail. Dad and I had some plugs. They imitated small fish that bass feed on. Brightly painted, two inches long, they had names designed to catch fishermen, like Jitter-Doodle and Hula Shaker. They filled tackle shop display cases, and their manufacturers were the magazine's biggest advertisers. Dad and I had succumbed to the fantasy and bought a few but had never caught a fish on one. After a few fruitless casts, we always untied the plug and reverted to the old standby, a worm on a hook.

But we had never fished a pond like this. It could be the chance of a lifetime, and Dad was not letting it slip by: "Would you mind if my boy and I tried fishing your pond?"

"Of course not. But you'd better prepare for the worst."

We did. We brought scythes, axes, and gas-powered chainsaws. We also brought thick rubber hip boots and a snakebite kit.

It really was a jungle. Trees were so overgrown with vines that we could not see their trunks. Poison ivy, half a foot wide at the base, wound completely around trees like mythical giant snakes that could have swallowed us whole. We encountered real snakes, too. They were probably not venomous, but we jumped as if they were.

Reeds and brambles were shoulder-high. Thorns penetrated our skin and stayed there. We were human pin cushions.

Pursuing our dream, we chain-sawed and hacked for hours. When we finally reached the pond, we were thrilled: it looked exactly like the ones on the covers. Water lilies the size of dinner plates rose above bright green pads so broad they covered the surface. Bullfrogs basked on them, patiently waiting for bugs to approach. They seemed to be smiling. Dragonflies hovered and darted miraculously. We felt a thousand miles from the city.

Now it was time for action.

I opened a tackle box full of plugs. They had lured us; surely, they would appeal to bass. Dad suggested a Wildwood Wrangler. Good choice. Its jointed center allowed both ends to swivel freely. With a twitch of the line, a skilled angler could make it look like an injured baitfish.

Such finesse proved unnecessary. No sooner had it touched the surface than the water exploded.

From beneath a lily pad, a monster bass had ambushed the lure--just as it was supposed to do. The fish rocketed straight up, landed on its side, and then rose again on its tail, all the while vigorously tossing its head from side to side to throw the hook. A series of leaps took it five feet across the water. What a show! We congratulated ourselves: the investment in plugs had finally paid off.

The fishing was like that for an hour, one furious bass after another. We surprised our host with six fish for his skillet, and his wife cooked us a feast fit for heroes.

We returned the following week full of anticipation but fished patiently for hours without a nibble. Belatedly, it dawned on us: the pond was too small to support more apex predators than we had removed. We had caught and cooked them all.

Many years later, I made a pilgrimage to Montana to learn fly fishing. There, to preserve the bounty of the great trout streams, the rule was "catch and release." You caught a trophy trout, photographed it cradled in your arms—they were huge – then freed it to fight again.

In the Baltimore of our time, even had we heard of the practice, we could not have imagined following it. We fishermen were like primordial hunters, out for meat and blood. Who would go to the expense and effort of pursuing prey without killing and eating it? Certainly not us.

Fishing was a gauge of how much time Dad had for me. He loved his work and stayed at it many evenings and weekends. I never had as much time with him as I wanted. I especially valued the time we spent fishing, just the two of us away from the world.

After he retired, I got an inkling that he had felt the same.

 I was taking him and Mom for a drive in the country. Mr. Teril was long gone, his estate a housing development. We had to drive farther out, way past the thoroughbred pastures of his former neighbors, to get a taste of the peace we had known. From the back seat, my father muttered something.

"What was that, Dad?" Out of the blue, without a preface of any kind, my father softly mused, "I should have taken you fishing more often."

4.
Down Home with William Faulkner

It was March 1961. I was completing my second year at the University of Chicago and enduring my second grim Chicago winter. On the calendar, it was spring and time for a two-week break from classes, but it was still bitterly cold and gray. Winter was endless.

Chicago was a city of heavy industry, the Rust Belt before it rusted. Steel mills, refineries, and stockyards operated around the clock, releasing dark clouds of smoke, which later drifted down as black soot. When I first observed it on new-fallen snow, I thought of black pepper on mashed potatoes. It was an amusing fancy, I thought. I was not amused for long. As the grains kept falling, they merged into a crust that left little white showing. My metaphor was no longer apt, and I was faced with a disturbing fact: the air I was breathing had turned pure snow black. What was it doing to my lungs?

The air also smelled bad. Each industry emitted a unique odor. To the west were stockyards and meat packing plants. If the wind came from there, it brought the nauseating stench of offal. To the south and east were steel mills. A breeze from there was acrid and metallic, so strong I could taste it. Only air from the north was pure. Sweeping down from Canada over the open waters of Lake Michigan, it was untainted by industrial emissions, but the lake was a natural wind tunnel 300 miles long. As the frigid Canadian air traveled its length unobstructed, it gained momentum. By the time it reached the southernmost shore, where the university was, it had often become a howling gale.

I experienced one of these storms my first winter in Chicago. I had an early morning class and stepped outside my dormitory to see what the weather was like. The wind was roaring in from the lake, driving sheets of snow and sleet parallel to the earth. It was snowing horizontally. Leaning into the wind, I trudged on. Icy crystals pummeled my face and penetrated the skin. I seemed to feel each one that struck like a dart—and my face was the dart board. The pain ceased when my face went numb from the cold—it was 15 degrees F.--but I was nearly blind, eyelids caked in ice, and could not speak through frozen lips. Staggering back to the dorm, I skipped class and went back to sleep.

I decided to head south for spring break to get warm, and my friend Rich agreed to join me. I had met him the previous year as a freshman. At nineteen, he was a year older but seemed infinitely wiser. A native of Chicago, the climate did not bother him, but he had never been anywhere else. I, on the other hand, was a lover of history and had driven through my native Maryland and neighboring Virginia and Pennsylvania, visiting historic sites.

Dad bought me my own car when I got my driver's license at sixteen. It was a '55 Chevy, white and turquoise, a color scheme in fashion that one model year. I didn't mind. Its scarcity made it easier to find in a parking lot. I immediately drove to Philadelphia to see Independence Hall.

Now, it was 1961, the centennial of the Civil War, and I wanted to see the Old South. New Orleans was due south, and getting there would take us to magnificent antebellum mansions in Natchez and Vicksburg, Mississippi. Besides, it was warm there. Spring had arrived in New Orleans weeks ago; its azaleas, camellias, and magnolias were in full bloom. Rather than wait for spring to come to us, we would go to it: to New Orleans.

The Interstate Highway System was just getting started. Here and there was a mile of brand-new freeway displaying a strange kind of route number, but the road would abruptly end without going anywhere. We had to use the old U.S. routes, which led us through the crowded center of every town. Progress was slow and plodding, but we got to see places the new freeways would bypass. Had we made the trip a few years later, we would not have known what we had missed. It was a last chance to see the country close up.

The farther south we drove, the warmer the day and the greener the foliage. As we had hoped, we were seeing spring unfold early.

We entered Mississippi around nine at night. We had finally reached the Deep South. The first small town we entered had prepared an official welcome. A white sedan pulled up behind us, a red light flashing, and the driver waved us off the road. He was not in uniform, but the word "Sheriff" was painted on the door inside an iconic five-starred badge. He parked beside us, slowly ambled over, and peered in.

My first time in the South, I thought he was greeting us. "Hello, officer, how are you tonight?"

"I am fine, thankya, but y'all been speedin'."

"Really? How fast was I going?"

"Twenty-two miles per hour. The speed limit is 20."

While he wrote the ticket for "speeding," Rich and I turned away. We were afraid of making each other laugh at this bumpkin from central casting. Rich had better control and politely thanked him while I prepared to drive off, but the sheriff called to us from his car: "Y'all follow me."

"Where?"

"To the J.P."

Rich turned to me: "What's a J.P.?"

I drew on my experience as a world traveler: "Trouble. The initials stand for Justice of the Peace, a kind of judge—a bad one for us in a place like this.

Our lawman led us to an imposing private home. The courtroom was a finely paneled room off the dining room. It had shelves like a library, but the only volumes they held were the Mississippi State Code and the Bible.

The room was luxuriously furnished, with genuine leather armchairs.

Rich whispered: "I bet he got all this with fines from the Yankees."

He was catching on. Our trial was brief and costly. Luckily, we had enough cash; if we had not, they would gladly have detained us in jail.

Chastened, I tried driving more slowly. I kept an eye on the speedometer and Rich on the rear-view mirror. Though our speed climbed again to 22 mph, we felt safe. There were no other cars on the road, and the next town's business center was the Dixie Diner, which was closed. But sure enough, lurking in the parking lot, hidden by hedges, was the next sheriff. He was much like the first.

"Y'all know why I stopped you?"

"No sir," I lied.

"Y'all was over the speed limit."

Before Mississippi, I had no moving violations. So much for my clean record--if these Bozos cared enough to report me to Maryland, which I doubted. I suspected they would report it to no one and keep the proceeds themselves.

Handing me the citation, he returned to his car and waved, "Follow me."

The Old South was rapidly losing its charm.

This time, while palming the exorbitant fine, the JP added a taunt: "Now you boys won't have so much for those New Orleans whores."

Rich and I exchanged puzzled glances. We hadn't even thought of that.

Two citations were enough for one night. We found a motel and started fresh the next day on U.S. 61, as slow and meandering as the Mississippi River, whose east bank it hugged to New Orleans. In Vicksburg and Natchez, we saw the magnificent antebellum mansions of cotton planters. Then we saw the fields that had grown their cotton.

The soil was so rich it was black. Workers in the fields were picking cotton. This portion of U.S. 61 was called the Blues Highway for the many famous musicians and singers who were born there, usually in the type of ramshackle cabins that dominated the scene around us--the homes of the current field hands.

Photographs from the Civil War era showed slaves picking cotton in these same fields. Bandanas around their necks, they stuffed cotton bolls into burlap sacks slung from a shoulder. Men, women, and children shared the work.

The scene before us was exactly the same, down to the way the workers were dressed and the bags they carried. I could feel the burlap scratching my skin. There were still no modern tractors, only mule-drawn plows. The resemblance was uncanny.

We were not prepared for this encounter with history. It was too real. It was one thing to read about slavery and another to see the past so vividly mirrored in the present. Too little had changed. We would not have seen this from a freeway and could hardly believe we were seeing it then, a century after the Civil War.

In New Orleans, despite the judicial hint, we did not look for prostitutes, but we did visit a few Bourbon Street strip clubs. I was amazed. How could there be so many beautiful women in two small blocks? The mystery was solved when we spied the same women, half-naked, slyly entering each club in turn by the rear door. They were simply reshuffling the deck.

In New Orleans, I had my first drink. Since Rich was sophisticated, I got what he ordered. It was tall and pink, with cherries on toothpicks, and looked like fruit punch. I gulped it down. Twenty minutes later, the women were even more attractive.

We found the warmth and sunshine we had craved and saw the attractions. My favorites were the ironwork balconies and the

Museum of the Confederacy, which had a life mask of Napoleon Bonaparte. He really was small.

To our surprise, we found travel through Mississippi more interesting than New Orleans itself. For variety, we took a different route back to Chicago. A two-lane state road took us through a crossroads with the tiniest church I ever saw, gleaming white in the morning sun. It was Sunday, and the congregation was just going in. We decided to join them. The young, good-looking minister gave a sermon with a minimal amount of fire and brimstone. When he came outside to greet each worshipper by name, he had by his side a sexy young woman. She looked like a Hollywood starlet. Apparently, preaching the Gospel had its earthly rewards.

Among the congregation were two diminutive, white-haired ladies who looked like sisters. In a refined southern accent I found charming, with wonderfully sweet smiles, they said how pleased they were we had taken time from our journey to join them. Other congregants came over one by one to say the same. We found this kind of friendliness and courtesy to be nearly ubiquitous in the state. It seemed to confirm the reputed gentility of southern life. We also saw signs, "Whites Only," posted at water fountains and bathrooms, reflecting another side of life in the South.

The road took us to Oxford, the home of William Faulkner, who used it as the setting for novels Rich and I had studied in Literature 101. No sooner had we passed the sign welcoming us to town than the car started clanging, sputtering, and bucking like a bronco. We barely managed to limp into the Town Square and Rebel Chevrolet. A mechanic there said we needed a complete tune-up, which would take a couple of hours. We had not planned on being there, but since we were, we asked if Mr. Faulkner's home was nearby. It was about a mile away. We got directions and started walking. Perhaps we'd get some insight into his writing.

On the way, we got further directions from a woman tending her garden. She knew Mr. Faulkner well, she said because her grandaddy and he were old fishing buddies. He was quiet and very private, almost shy: "You would never guess he wrote all those long books."

She had already taught us more about Mr. Faulkner than we had learned from our course.

She told us that he was teaching at the University of Virginia, but she thought that in his absence, we could get permission to look around his home.

When we got there, we saw no one around. There was no fence or gate, simply a long colonnade of tall, somewhat spindly trees. They were draped in a ghostly shroud of Spanish moss. We walked down the path to find someone to ask and got a good look at the house. Built in the Greek revival style of the mansions at Natchez, the house looked a little run down--in need of more revival. This was not Natchez, and this was no mansion. It was much smaller and simpler, antebellum and historic, but unpretentious. It was surprisingly modest, we thought, for a person of Mr. Faulkner's stature.

It was dwarfed by tall cedars and pines. The ground beneath their limbs was hard and bare; deep shade prevented anything from growing there. The scene was as gloomy as a Faulkner novel.

We saw an elderly black man slowly pushing a wheelbarrow of mulch. I called to him:

"Good day, sir. Is it all right if we look around?"

"You have to ask Mr. Faulkner."

We knew he was in Virginia, but I asked anyway:

"Where would we find him?"

"He in there," he said, with a nod towards the house.

"In where?"

"In th' house."

I was puzzled, but apparently, there was SOME kind of Faulkner in there—perhaps a relative who was minding the house in his absence. We would ask him. I stepped onto the creaky, uneven planks of the porch and knocked. Rich stayed ten feet behind.

The front door opened, and the screen door cast a gauzy shadow on the face of the occupant. He was an older brother or perhaps an uncle. He bore a definite familial resemblance to the dashing, handsome author on the jacket of "The Sound and the Fury" but was too old and short to be Mr. Faulkner himself. I was 5 feet six, and he was no taller. The man in the photo was tall.

Quietly, in the refined Southern accent of the church ladies, he said, "Good evenin'."

I could not reply in kind at two in the afternoon, so I simply said, "Hello, sir. I am sorry to bother you, but your groundskeeper said to ask you if we could look around."

He replied softly, "This is private property."

Then the penny dropped. I suddenly realized that this was the author himself. The photo on the book jacket had been taken years ago when he was young. His supposed height was a trick of the camera. I was seeing the updated Mr. Faulkner.

"Of course, sir, I am sorry to have disturbed you."

I turned to leave, but before Mr. Faulkner could close the front door, my colleague to the rear, erstwhile mute, blurted a bold-faced lie:

"But we came all the way from Chicago just to see you." What a whopper. Lying to a Nobel Laureate! I think I blushed.

"This is private property," he repeated, still softly.

Sheepishly, we departed.

The University of Mississippi was close by, just across the road from the entrance to the colonnade. As we emerged from the trees, a convertible full of young men was leaving the campus. As they turned onto the road between the campus and the Faulkner home, they stopped, and the driver called out: "Hi there, fellas. How ya doin'?"

"Fine, thank you. How are you? We just saw Mr. Faulkner," I advised.

"You don't say? Did you have a nice chat?"

"No, he wouldn't talk with us."

"Oh, he'll talk with you. Just tell him I sent you. I'm his Cousin Willy. Tell him Cousin Willy sent you."

Rich came alive: "Thank you. That's very nice of you!"

What luck! Emboldened, we retraced our way up the dark drive to the front door. At least I did. My friend was still ten feet behind.

I hesitated. I had my doubts about Cousin Willy, particularly since the car had sped away, tires screeching, right after our chat. But once more, I knocked.

I didn't say a word, but again, ever so mildly, in that genteel accent, he repeated, "This is private property."

That was more than enough for me; I felt like a total fool. But my friend to the rear got renewed courage: "Your Cousin Willy sent us."

Had he really said that? Anyone else might have been furious and shown it, but Mr. Faulkner remained the soul of courtesy and quietly repeated, "This is private property."

I felt terrible. As we trudged down the path once more, Rich seemed finally to see the light. He shrewdly observed: "That guy was no Cousin Willie; he tricked us." How could someone so mature and wise be so naive? Then again, I was the one who knocked.

On the walk back to Rebel Chevrolet, we again passed the lady in her garden. We told her whom we had seen. "Oh, I remember now. His wife had surgery, and he came back from Virginia to take care of her. Otherwise, he never would have answered the door. He is very private."

We could confirm that. We didn't mention Cousin Willy.

To this day, I am impressed with the way Mr. Faulkner managed the situation. Considering what the garden lady told us about his wife, it could not have been easy having two bumbling idiots on his doorstep. Yet he remained a gentleman.

Little more than a year later, in July 1962, Mr. Faulkner died of complications from a riding accident. He was 64. I was sad to learn of it and regretted our thoughtless behavior.

The car was ready as promised. We drove off and soon came to one of those tiny stretches of freeway bearing a new Interstate badge number. It extended only five miles, just long enough for us to be tagged for speeding a third time.

This time, it was not a local sheriff but a state trooper. Unlike the sheriffs, he wore a neat uniform and was courteous.

"Now you boys know why I had to stop you, don't you?"

Not really. I was doing 52 in a 50-mph zone, but I liked his manner, so I met him halfway: "I was going too fast?"

"Just a little, but the law is the law."

We girded for the third JP, but the trooper simply handed us the ticket and said, "Take this to the nearest Justice of the Peace." He did not ask us to follow him and, tipping his cap, drove off.

 "What?" I asked Rich. "On our own? Without an official escort?" State police apparently had a higher code than local sheriffs.

There was no judicial address on the ticket, and the trooper had not given us one, so we didn't know where the J.P. was. I don't think his heart was in it. I doubt he expected us to go looking for this character just to receive more rough justice. We decided to make a run for it.

Still, there was the risk of running afoul of the Fugitive Slave Law or whatnot. We could spend years in a Mississippi jail or on the chain gangs we saw on the roads, pounding stones with sledgehammers in the broiling sun. We wouldn't last long.

I had a plan. My parents had mailed my annual new Maryland license plates from Baltimore before we left. The old ones had not quite expired, so I had tossed the new ones in the trunk. They bore a different number. This seemed the perfect time to make the switch, and we replaced last year's with the new ones. Now, even if the trooper was distressed by our failure to appear in court and sent an all-points bulletin to every drooling sheriff in the state, they would never find us. They would be looking for plates with the old numbers. The perfect crime. No, not a crime; simply payback for two injustices of the peace.

Our escape was uneventful.

5.
Accidental Activism

In April 1962, I had just spent my second freezing winter at the University of Chicago, a fine university in a poor climate. I had grown up farther south, in Baltimore, and was used to spring coming on time, not three weeks late. It was still a bit cold for my taste, but I was current in all my courses. Why not take off a week or so? I had always wanted to see the Florida Everglades. Why not now?

I could have headed for beaches with girls rather than swamps with alligators. I was inexperienced with both but less afraid of the reptiles.

As it happened, I had a talkative female passenger as far as Atlanta. Catherine "Kit" Plom was the charismatic diva of our local chapter of the Young People's Socialist League. Members called themselves "YPSLs," pronounced YIP-sills, and were not as radical as their name implied. They-advocated Democratic Socialism. Most of their proposals, like national health, had already been in place for years in Western Europe. Others, like Medicare, were soon adopted here too.

Still, I never officially joined. This was the height of the Cold War, when many equated Socialism with Communism, and I didn't want to be tarred with the same brush. My involvement was limited to attending a series of lectures they sponsored and having informal discussions over coffee.

A more active member was the future Senator Bernie Sanders. He transferred to the university when I had been there for a year. Kit introduced us then: "This is Bernie; he's from Brooklyn." I did not get to know him. I did not even remember meeting him until decades later when he ran for president. Then photos of him as a young civil rights activist appeared in the press, and I recognized him as the same Bernie. He was still a YPSL.

Kit, like Bernie, was active in the civil rights movement. She was one of the "Freedom Riders" who worked to integrate interstate buses by riding on them, often at great personal risk. A true crusader, she carried copies of her arrest records and mug shots with her at all times. She proudly showed them to me the first time we met. I had never encountered anyone like her.

It was in connection with those activities that I gave her a ride to Atlanta. Shortly before my departure for the swamps, I ran into her on campus. I mentioned I would miss the next lecture because I would be driving to Florida.

"Are you going through Atlanta?"

"Yes, I have to. Why?

"When will you be getting there?"

I gave her the date, and she was beside herself.

"Unbelievable! That is exactly when I have to be there."

"Be there for what?"

She wanted to attend the first organizing conference of a brand new civil rights organization, the Student Non-Violent Coordinating Committee, or SNCC. It was being held at Atlanta University, a leading black college.

"I can take you."

Kit talked all the way. She explained that the young blacks who had organized the conference were close to Martin Luther King. They had been practicing his principles of civil disobedience at lunch counters throughout the South.

She aroused my curiosity. When I dropped her off, I asked the student hosts if I could remain. They said they would be pleased to have me and moved a cot into the room of two students with a bunk bed, who graciously offered it to me. Of course, I declined. Others drifted in, and we all ordered pizza. We stayed awake late that night, getting to know each other.

The students were all African-American, but I felt totally at home. My new friends welcomed me warmly and patiently explained their movement.

As they saw it, when an oppressor has overwhelming power, violence is not the answer. A peaceful sit-in is the better tactic.

I understood all that. What mystified me was how they found the courage to face armed mobs and snarling dogs.

On the first day of the meeting, I noticed a distinguished-looking gentleman, middle-aged and very white, smiling and taking photos of everyone. I guessed he was from the FBI and decided not to sign the list of attendees. Based on subsequent revelations of FBI surveillance, I was probably correct. They had my picture but not my name.

This was SNCC's first organizational conference, where a young John Lewis was elected its first chairman.

I confirmed this decades later when I met him at a reception in Washington. He was Congressman Lewis then, having represented his district in Atlanta for years.

When I told him I had been at the conference, he positively beamed with joy. I did not tell him I was there by accident.

By then, he was widely known and respected as a preeminent civil rights activist. His rise to that status began the year after the SNCC conference when he helped Martin Luther King arrange the historic March on Washington. At 23, he was the youngest keynote speaker at that event. Later that day, Dr. King delivered his "I have a dream" speech.

I was there, but this time my attendance was no accident. Since the SNCC conference, I have followed developments closely. I did not have the courage to demonstrate myself, but I could show my support by joining the crowd on the Mall--the largest the capital had ever seen.

John Lewis died in July 2020. On the day of his memorial service, I was spending my second day in hospital. My heart had begun an altercation with the rest of me, and I was waiting for it to settle down. The nurses told me the condition wasn't serious but that I had to rest until my heart rate returned to normal.

While I was resting and waiting, there was a TV in the room, and I watched the hours-long memorial ceremony, which CNN covered free of commercials. I heard eulogies that sent chills down my spine, delivered by preachers and orators of immense power. They echoed the spirituality I first experienced in Atlanta.

God bless Kit, whatever, and wherever she is protesting now. There are two photos of her on my desk, one frontal, one profile – her Alabama State Police mug shots.

Postscript

I proceeded to the Everglades, but after Atlanta, the experience could only be anticlimactic. I didn't know there was a dry season, but I was in it, and the swamps held much less life than I had expected. However, I did encounter some wildlife as I was leaving the Everglades: I ran over an alligator. It was sunning itself motionless on the black asphalt road, and I thought it was a heat mirage until I felt the thump-thump of my left front and rear tires as they rolled over it. They left a deep indentation where the tail joined the body, but the wounded animal dragged itself into the brush and disappeared. I considered turning back to see how it was doing but thought better of it.

The return to Chicago was otherwise uneventful.

6.
Fellow Travelers

LONDON

I first met Daphne near Buckingham Palace. I was there early in the morning, hoping to see the changing of the guard, but I couldn't find the palace. Beyond the Iron Gate, in the distance, was a nondescript government building but no palace. I scanned the waiting crowd for someone to ask. I didn't want another tourist who would be equally clueless. I needed a local resident.

Then I saw her nibbling fish and chips from a cone of grease-soaked newspaper. That was how street vendors served them, wrapped in newsprint. She had to be British.

"Pardon me, Madam. Where is Buckingham Palace."

She stared at me queerly. "It's right there, love."

She was pointing to the government building.

"Oh. I didn't recognize it."

"It is rather plain, isn't it? Not what a palace should be."

She was definitely English, her speech soft and precise, her movements quick as a bird, and considerate, putting me at ease for my mistake. Her slightly graying hair was drawn back in a bun, but as she spoke, a few strands slipped free onto her brow. She tried brushing them back with one hand while juggling her food with the other. "Drat. I need a third hand."

"Let me help you."

Handing me the cone, she tucked in the wayward hair. "How rude of me. Take some if you like."

I handed it back. My hand was greasy, and I wiped it on my pants discreetly. I didn't want to offend her. Likewise, I tried not to wince at the prospect of eating the proffered food. "No, thanks. I'd like to have breakfast first."

"Didn't your bed-and-breakfast provide one?"

"I don't have a b-and-b. I am homeless."

"Oughtn't you be looking for one?"

"Yes, I will be shortly. I headed here to see a bit of London before the ordeal."

"You poor boy. We must find you a place before they fill up. I am Daphne. Come with me."

"I am Steve, but where are we going?"

"Russell Square. It has the best selection. Hurry."

I didn't ask why she was volunteering; I was glad for the help. We dashed to the nearest Tube station, and on the train, I filled her in. It was June 1965, the start of my summer vacation from graduate school. My university in Boston had chartered flights to and from London. Between the two, I would have ten weeks to tour Europe. On a tight budget, my guidebook was "Europe on Five Dollars a Day." Unfortunately, everyone else had the same book. When I arrived at London's Heathrow Airport the night before, I phoned every b-and-b in the book, but other tourists had gotten there first; there were no vacancies. The only room I could find was in a luxury establishment, White's Hotel. I hurried there before that, too, was gone.

Bedraggled from the flight and lacking a coat and tie, I was not as well dressed as the doorman. I was afraid he would not let me in. As I was slinking through the elegant lobby a bellhop in livery offered to add my luggage to a shiny brass cart. All I had was the nylon knapsack on my back. Placing it atop the monogrammed leather suitcases on the cart would have been embarrassing. "Thank you, but I can manage." I felt like a thumb in a punchbowl.

The porter who showed me to my room could have played a duke or an earl in an old English movie. The room itself was cavernous, a size I never heard of-- a "triple." It had three beds side by side, with enough room for three more. The bathroom was correspondingly huge, with a mahogany-paneled marble bathtub so deep I could immerse myself completely, head and all. I lay there underwater, blowing bubbles to the surface. Climbing out, I could have used a ladder.

I had an acute sense of being too poor to belong there, but everyone treated me with deference. Perhaps they thought the occupant of such a room must be important. More likely, like most Londoners I encountered, they were simply being courteous.

I had nightmares of penury. Having spent too much on my first night in London, I was washing dishes to pay a restaurant check. Then, sleeping on a park bench, I was arrested for vagrancy. I woke twice in a cold sweat.

In the morning, I paid for two unoccupied beds and myself and quickly left. The atmosphere was so rich I was afraid they might charge me for breathing the air.

Daphne listened sympathetically. "You poor boy. We'll get you properly situated."

She knew the owner of an excellent, reasonably priced b-and-b. Gratefully, I checked in. Though I had not spent the night, the proprietor graciously gave me the breakfast that went with the bed. My first English breakfast was three times the size of an American dinner. Daphne only had tea, but when she thought no one was looking, I spied her pilfering bits of sausage from my plate. I would gladly have ordered her some, but she apparently preferred encroaching on mine. I found her mischief endearing.

"Daphne, this is very kind of you, but don't you have to be at work?"

"I have the week off. They are taking inventory. But I wanted to pay you back."

"For what?"

"I knew you were American before you spoke from your honesty. Take the Frenchman. He pretends to be sophisticated, never at a loss. You were bewildered, and you showed it. You Americans are open and unpretentious. That's what I love about you."

"You love us because we are guileless?"

"That, and because you saved us from Hitler. I lived through the Blitz."

"You are too young."

"I am old enough, believe me."

"When you smile, you look like a schoolgirl."

She tried to hide her blush, but it was classic, bright red.

"Flatterer!" she admonished, obviously flattered. "Imagine my gratitude when you lot joined in. What did the French ever do for us?"

Wondering about her negativity toward France, I had to concede that America had done more for the war effort.

"I had nothing to do with that. I was a child during the war.

"Was your father in the service?"

"The Army. He came home safe."

"He might not have done. He risked his life for us."

She placed a hand on mine. I had to suppress a smile. It was the hand she had used to raid my plate; it retained a trace of larcenous sausage grease.

"Let me show you my London."

"I couldn't let you do that. We just met."

"Yes, but I've been waiting for years to repay America."

I could not dissuade her. She did agree to let me pay for meals and admission fees. She even balked at that, but I insisted.

We were in the Bloomsbury district, near the British Museum. We began our tour there. Attic to the world, it had everything. We marveled at the immense collection of ancient Greek vases. There were so many we wondered how there could be any left in Greece. We stared at the Elgin Marbles, the frieze from the Parthenon. Its three-dimensional depiction of life in ancient Athens was incredibly realistic, and I could understand why the governments of modern Greece and the United Kingdom were disputing its ownership. Greece claimed it had been stolen and wanted it back. We enjoyed it while we could before it got moved again.

In this preeminent institution, of all places, I realized that Britain's standard of living was not up to par. The clue was its toilet paper. The roll in the British Museum men's room was so coarse it contained flecks of wood. I was afraid of getting splinters. When I mentioned this to Daphne, she reminded me that food rationing had ended only eleven years earlier, nine years after the War was over. I apologized.

We decided to bypass some of the usual tourist sites in favor of an insider's tour. She suggested Regent's Park Zoo, popular with English families. Though modest, it did have a resident celebrity, Guy the Gorilla. He had been there since 1947. He was huge, and his appearance was fearsome, but he was famous for being gentle. According to Daphne, when small birds flew into his cage, he cradled them in his hands, quietly examined them, and then let them alight from his massive fingers. Fearing she was pulling my leg, I confirmed the account from reliable sources. Guy was immensely popular with the British public, many of whom sent greeting cards each year on his birthday.

We spent a while observing him, and he us, with a strangely human, quizzical gaze, but no birds entered his cage, which was sadly bare and primitive for such an exceptional creature. The zoo, like the British Museum, seemed underfunded.

However, it had one attraction I had never seen before: camel rides. Mothers ascended a kind of saddle; then attendants passed up their wriggling offspring. We followed the course of ten children. Four laughed with joy; three burst out crying, and three remained silent, waiting to see how things turned out. We wagered on each child, but neither of us predicted the crying mother, apparently petrified to be so high off the ground on a swaying platform. I saw no foreign tourists. It was a local family affair.

The Tower of London was mandatory and crowded, but Daphne had inside information. "Let me show you something," she said, tugging me by the sleeve away from the crowd. Among the exhibits on a lower floor, she pointed to a gleaming suit of armor, standing straight and tall as if its owner were still wearing it. "Can you guess who that belonged to?" As she asked, she blocked with her hand the printed exhibit card with the answer.

"How would I know?"

"What if I told you Henry VIII?"

"I'd say it was too small."

She removed her hand. "Go ahead, read it."

She was right. It belonged to Henry, but before, he grew fat when he was young and athletic. I asked Daphne why the king's full-sized armor was not there, too. She pointed to a nearby case. There was obese Henry's armor. He had grown from a Large to a XXX-Large.

I might have missed that, but for her impish delight in incongruities, which included our common language. One day, at a Tube station, we had to go to a higher level. "Where is the elevator operator?" I asked. She laughed out loud.

"What's so funny?"

"You mean, "Lift attendant.""

"No, I parried."

"You do. I would never use such a silly expression."

Another station had an unusual escalator. Not only was it the steepest I had ever seen, it was constructed entirely of wood. A carpenter's delight of perfectly meshed parts, it was a work of art. I asked my friend why that material had been used. "Was there a metal shortage?"

"I don't know. Ask one of your 'elevator operators.'" At that, she could not stop giggling."

Daphne excelled at Westminster Abbey. She knew where everyone was buried, saving time searching for favorites. It felt odd, though, to be walking over some of them. More interesting to me was the building next door, which housed the British Parliament. I wanted to observe a debate in the House of Commons.

This was a tradition with me. I grew up in Baltimore, an hour's drive from the Capitol Building in Washington. When I turned sixteen and got a driver's license, I occasionally skipped school to observe Congress in session. It was simple. I parked free on the street and walked a block to the Capitol. Security was unobtrusive, and I could wander freely. I might share an elevator with a congressman or Senator. The visitors' gallery was never crowded. I sat in the first row, practically next to whoever had the floor.

I wanted to repeat the experience in the Mother of Parliaments, and Daphne got us tickets. As it happened, it was June 25, 1965, the date of a historic debate. At issue was the Abolition of Hanging Act, which replaced the death penalty for murder with a mandatory life sentence.

Daphne had been closely following the news and filled me in. The proponent of the bill was a long-time Labour MP, Sydney

Silverman, who had advocated abolition for decades. His bill was being debated, and he spoke on its behalf. Daphne said he was one of the foremost orators in England.

Listening closely to him, I thought I heard a touch of the accent employed by British actors when portraying Jewish characters, such as Shakespeare's Shylock or Dickens' Fagan. I asked Daphne, who said I was right. The M.P. had been born in poverty to immigrant Jewish parents in Liverpool. My father's background was similar; he was born to immigrant Jewish parents in Baltimore. He had become a successful lawyer and a player in Maryland politics, though nowhere near Mr. Silverman's level. I was pleased that the UK, reputedly divided along lines of class, had offered the same opportunity for advancement as our country, which allegedly was not.

The debate was followed by a comic vignette, a "division of the House." Members filed out of the chamber, some to the left, others to the right. "Are they going home?" I asked Daphne.

"No. They are voting."

In the Congress, members remained in place for a vote, but here, the ayes and nays went to designated locations to register their vote. Then they paraded back in to hear the results. All the coming and going looked silly to me, but to them it was tradition, always important in England.

Later that year, I learned that Mr. Silverman's act passed by a large majority.

By week's end, we'd had enough sightseeing, and Daphne invited me to her home in Surrey. I met her neighbors, a young couple with a charming little girl, six-year-old Alison. She spoke with the clarity of a BBC anchorperson, enunciating each word in a refined British accent. Mark Twain said children in France were so bright they knew how to speak French. Alison spoke BBC.

I thanked Daphne and gave her a gold locket with a photo of us together. Then I showed her a telegram my father wrote when I told him about her: "Dear Daphne, I appreciate your gratitude for my wartime service. You have more than repaid me with your kindness to my son. God bless you. And God save the Queen."

"Nice touch, Dad." She shed a few tears, while I tried not to and we hugged a long time. Then I was off to Paris.

PARIS

The boat train to Paris had three links: train from London to Dover, ferry across the Channel, and train to Paris. It was a grueling overnight journey. In the morning, the train pulled into a station I recognized from Monet's many paintings of it, an auspicious beginning. From there, I boarded the Metro, which was amazingly smooth and silent. Every other subway I had ridden had screeching steel wheels. This one had rubber tires.

I headed for my lodging. After my experience in London, I made advance reservations at a budget hotel. On the way, I got off at the Champs-Elysées. Before dealing with a mundane room, I wanted a glimpse of Paris. From the dimly lit Metro, I ascended into the brilliant morning sunshine. I also was enveloped by the scent of flowers, but there were none in sight. It was perfume. The air was full of it. There was nothing like that in London, and the ladies wearing it were different too. Sleek and fashionable, they walked with a style and confidence I had not seen anywhere else. I was wearing the clothes I wore in London, where they were acceptable, but now I felt underdressed. I was unfashionable in the capital of fashion.

I disdained the world of designers, models, and runways and feared I would not be comfortable there, but my hotel was on the Bohemian Left Bank, where people dressed as they pleased; the worse, the better. I fit right in.

Though inexpensive, my hotel was only two blocks from the Sorbonne, which offered day trips by bus to Chartres Cathedral. I watched passing fields of wheat, from which the cathedral suddenly appeared, rising from the plain.

To medieval travelers it must have seemed a miraculous beacon, but I thought it would have been more impressive had its two towers matched. They were of different heights and styles. Never mind, they were finished years apart; to me, they looked lopsided.

This was my first experience of French Gothic architecture; once inside the structure, my carping criticism fell away. The vaulted ceiling soared. It lifted me, not to heaven, as the builders had intended, but closer than I had ever been before.

The façade of the cathedral was dominated by stone sculptures of holy figures. Their limbs and torsos were preternaturally elongated, a distortion of reality that gave them an other-worldly authority. The cathedral was most renowned for its resplendent stained-glass windows. They were truly stunning. Having experienced the esthetic power of this magnificent building, as I walked back to the bus, I shot a glance over my shoulder. Some gremlin inside me persisted: "If only the towers matched."

The Sorbonne also offered French lessons, for which I signed up, but I could not sit in a classroom with all of Paris before me. Nor could I stay confined to a museum. The Louvre was full to the brim with tourists. I could see crowds viewing the Mona Lisa but not the painting itself. Instead, I viewed less popular masterpieces. But I wanted to be outside, walking the avenues and promenades.

In that regard, Paris had something for which I was grateful: the pissoir. This was a painted steel cylinder, a kiosk, its exterior plastered like any other with notices and ads for concerts, but with a walk-in entrance. There was no door. You simply entered and kept walking until you reached the urinal. For that's what it was: a public urinal. You were concealed from passing pedestrians from the calf up, but all the world could see your shoes. Those on the outside counted feet to see how long they would have to wait. Pissoirs were easy to find. If you approached a kiosk that smelled of urine, you had found one.

Before I discovered the pissoir, walking in Paris was an ordeal. When nature called, which was often on inexpensive wine, I had to find a restaurant, implore the manager in broken French to use the bathroom, and then, if allowed, wind my way slowly past crowded tables. If my progress was too slow, or if the bathroom was occupied, I might pee in my pants. The pissoir eliminated that strife. It occurred to me, though, that while the French took care of their men, its women were on their own.

On a higher note, I found romance in Paris. Shortly before Bastille Day, I met a young woman, Helene, at an outdoor café. She was lively, with a charming accent, and we got along well. She was, of all things, German. I was ethnically Jewish. Though not religious, I was aware that Germans of the prior generation, perhaps even her parents, had not always drawn fine distinctions. We didn't discuss politics, but she didn't strike me as a practitioner of genocide. She was a secretary for an American corporation and spoke excellent English. I liked her.

We got a taste of French joie de vie on Bastille Day. That night, the city was deluged with showers, thunder, and blinding lightning. At the same time, a fireworks show was in progress. After each barrage of fireworks, the crowd uttered a cry of appreciation, "Oo La La." They began doing the same after each flash of lightning. It became a game played from under the waterlogged awnings of sidewalk cafes. In rhythm with natural and artificial explosions, laughter flowed from the crowd in waves.

Later that night, at Helene's flat, her radio was tuned to a German station. The music was pleasant until midnight when lilting ballads were replaced by the blaring tones of "Deutschland, Deutschland, Uber Alles," which I thought was a Nazi marching song. Sheepishly, I asked why that was being played.

"That is our national anthem."

Apparently, I was mistaken. I was inclined to believe her; the station was more likely signing off with the national anthem than with a Nazi marching song.

I put it out of my mind and squeezed into her tiny bed. Everything was tiny. Her flat was a garret, five flights up in a tenement. The single light bulb on each stairwell was controlled by a wall switch on an egg timer. No matter how fast I moved or where I was going, it buzzed audibly down to darkness before I got there. On her floor, that was either her flat or the "bathroom". Fortunately, they were far apart because the latter was a hole in the bare concrete floor. There was no toilet, no seat of any kind between the user and the contents of the pit below. English plumbing may have been old-fashioned, but this was unspeakable. After the toilet paper episode at the British Museum, however, 1 kept quiet. I tried to think the French were doing the best they could with what they had.

Our budding affections were thwarted on two fronts. First was her lack of faith in contraception. She was not opposed to it; she simply was not sure it would work and was afraid of having a "bebe." It sounded cute when she said it, but not so much when she adhered to it. With time, we might have gotten past that, but there remained the other obstacle: her Norwegian flatmate. Of all the nationalities I observed in Paris, the tallest were Norwegian. She towered over us and was always there. Even had my fraulein been willing, we could not have gotten far with this Viking hanging around. Consequently, I spent my nights in Paris cuddling affectionately. It could have been worse.

VENICE

In northern Europe, the weather tended towards gray and damp. I was ready for the South. I took an overnight express train to Venice. I got no sleep and went directly to bed. The next morning, I was wakened by an aria from La Boheme. Peering out the window to the canal below, I spied the tenor. He was one of the men collecting trash on a workboat. They were all smiling broadly in the sunshine, enjoying their work as much as his singing. This was my kind of place.

I was lost in Venice the whole week I was there. The canals were a maze I never got the hang of, but it didn't matter. It was all magical. Once, my aimless wanderings ended at a working-class bar. There,

I encountered the rarest people in Venice, permanent residents. Unlike their countrymen in the tourist districts, they spoke no English but warmly greeted me and treated me to a wine, then another. The city of fantasy and dreams had come alive with real people.

ROME

"Aqua non potabile." My new companion was reading aloud a notice above the wash basin. Pretending that translation was necessary, he enunciated deliberately, "Water … not …drinkable."

I was washing my face in the basin and, from the faucet, was gulping down water that, apparently, was not fit to drink. Robert watched bemused. "Too late now," he said. "Let's hope the water has healing properties."

It might have. We were in the Vatican. The men's room in the Vatican Museum was ornately decorated with expensive marble. I wished they had spent less on marble and more on plumbing. I was just getting to know Robert; I hoped he wasn't prone to schadenfreude, that untranslatable German word for delighting in others' misfortune. More likely, he simply saw the humor in the situation. Time will tell. We had met a few days ago at a Roman restaurant. Having dinner at separate tables, we found ourselves chatting, and he invited me to his, which had a better view of the piazza, the Campo di Fiore. The vendors of its open-air market had closed their stalls for the day. Now, it was evening, and Robert advised me it was time for the passagiata.

"What is that?" I asked. That was his cue. He was a professor of Italian at a southern college who spent his summers in Italy. A native of Georgia, his Italian had a southern drawl.

"That, my young friend, is when Italians take an evening stroll around the piazza to see what's going on. They greet friends and neighbors and talk until dark. It's done in every town in Italy." He spoke slowly and distinctly, as if to a class taking notes. I was in the class. I was getting the first of his lectures on Italy.

I was grateful. If he hadn't pointed it out to me, I might not have noticed the residents of all ages passing by in a stream, chattering away. When the train to Venice first entered Italy at a tiny station, I observed two men in a heated argument. There was much gesticulating and raising of voices. I was sure they would come to blows, especially when one called the other a "Bastard!" I was wrong. It was simply an Italian discussion. What I heard was "Basta," Italian for "enough." It meant that the conversation was over. They parted laughing. I was not surprised, therefore, when the passagiatta proved a noisy affair, punctuated for emphasis by hands constantly in motion. From then on, we had dinner and observed the spectacle together.

He was the perfect guide. From prior trips, he knew of things I would have missed completely, like outdoor operas at the Baths of Caracalla. Massive ruins were what remained of the largest bath complex in the Roman Empire. On summer nights they served as the backdrop for operas, attended by mainly Italian audiences. Many in the crowd knew the operas by heart; I could tell from the way they sang along.

Our first was Verdi's Aida. As the overture faded, the curtain rose, revealing a highly realistic mural. It depicted men of ancient Egypt beside a crouching camel. The brushwork on the camel was meticulous; the image was incredibly lifelike. Then, the painting moved. Slowly, the camel rose to its full height, and one of the men led it offstage. The audience roared and whistled its approval. I turned to Robert: "Did you know about the camel."

"It was a hit last year. I figured they'd do it again." The music was magnificent, but since the characters sang in Italian, I hadn't a clue what they were saying. Still, how about that camel?

The next night was Carmen. "Some say it is the best opera ever written," Robert informed me and proceeded to lecture me why. I preferred La Boheme, the one other opera I knew, but said nothing. He needed to be right more than I did. I didn't mind. I appreciated the information Robert imparted; I could overlook any pomposity that came with it.

We met each morning for breakfast to select a destination. It was August and Rome was having a heat wave, one hundred degrees day after day. We could not stand the trolleys, which were crowded, steamy, and unbelievably smelly. We walked everywhere. After a week, I had my shoes repaired. My guidebook said Rome had over 2,000 fountains, more than any other city in the world. We put them to good use. When we reached a fountain we splashed water on each other until our shirts were soaking wet. Evaporation kept us cool. By the time we reached the next fountain, never far, our shirts were completely dry, and we drenched them again.

The only hint of playfulness I saw in Robert was during a watering session. I caught him laughing as misdirected water flowed past my waist and down my pants. I suspected he would not have been so amused had they been his pants.

He made up for it with another gem of knowledge: some of the fountains, including the largest and most famous, the Trevi, were still supplied by ancient aqueducts. He showed me one. Pointing far into the distance, he traced its limestone towers, marching in pairs down the hills to Rome. From fresh mountain springs, through gravity alone, this structure had been bringing water to the city for two thousand years.

He also drew my attention to the portrait busts at the Capitoline Museum. They depicted ancient Roman emperors and luminaries, warts and all--literally. The sculptors revealed every imperfection-- warts, double chins, crooked noses, drooping lips. The busts portrayed real people. If the heads were on bodies in modern clothes, they would have blended right in with the Italians outside.

Robert and I suited each other. He was a born teacher, and I was a willing student. We parted amicably.

PROVENCE

After three weeks, I was ready to leave Rome for the Italian and French Rivieras. Just in time, I encountered Pierre, a fellow American of French origin. We met in a Roman pizzeria. A craving for Italian American food had overcome us both at the same time. As luck would have it, he was going my way to Provence. He was four years older but had a charming, childlike quality; there was a perpetual twinkle in his eye. A professor of French at a Vermont college, he too spent his summers in Europe. I could not afford a rental car and was resigned to seeing the coastal scenery by train, but Pierre had a car. I asked if I could ride with him. He was a jovial soul. "Certainly, my friend, come along." In return for half the expenses, I got the scariest ride of my life.

The hills above the French Riviera terrified me. Cars came speeding around blind curves on a road barely wide enough for one. Pierre had been there before and didn't mind, but I closed my eyes and prayed. When we finally descended the hills, I actually kissed the ground; I was surprised to be alive.

We came to the ground at Arles, where we visited the little house that Van Gogh shared with Gaugin. It was thrilling to see the real thing, including the bed and chair, exactly as he painted it. Later, someone told us the original had been destroyed in the war. They assured us, however, that it was an exact replica. It didn't matter. We didn't have to refund our initial excitement. Around the corner from the house, we had coffee at the café that Van Gogh frequented; it, too, looked as if he had painted it. We half expected him to drop by.

Pierre and I had similar tastes, reflected in what we chose not to see. Without stopping, we drove right by the casino at Monte Carlo and the fashionable beaches of Cannes and St. Tropez. We preferred two ancient structures near Arles. Both date from the first century A.D., around the time of the Colosseum. One was the tallest aqueduct bridge in the Roman Empire. With three levels of towering arches to provide the necessary height, it spanned a deep, rugged ravine. The other was one of the best-preserved arenas in the empire, still used for operas.

There were hardly any tourists at these sites. They were too busy crowding together on the narrow, rocky spits that passed for beaches on the Riviera. We didn't question their judgment but were glad they were somewhere else.

An art history professor claimed that Van Gogh exaggerated the colors of fields and meadows around Arles. That intensification of reality was the beginning of modern art. Seeing Provence for myself, I disagreed. I thought the vibrancy of his paintings reflected what he was actually seeing. Flooded in the sunshine, Provence itself was an exaggeration.

SPAIN

Pierre was more easygoing than Robert. He was less compelled to teach. I found I was asking questions rather than being given answers. We parted at the train station in Marseilles. He was going to Switzerland, and I was to Madrid. Before we boarded, however, he did me a huge favor. A colleague of his taught Spanish at his college and lived with her family in Madrid in the summer. He would ask if she could show me around.

He had a photograph. She was absolutely gorgeous. Thank you, Pierre! Unfortunately, she was not available, but she had an older sister. She was not physically attractive but was incredibly kind, and we had a lot of fun. We went to a bullfight and saw the actor Anthony Quinn in the stands. Everyone did. He stood his full height and drained a goatskin of wine to much applause. We went to an authentic flamenco club for some of the world's most exciting music.

The high point of my visit was spending a siesta with her family. Contrary to what I had believed, it was not a time of sleep, only of rest in the hottest part of the day. Her whole family welcomed me for a long lunch, including her middle-aged father, who came home from work for the occasion. While the residents of Madrid took two hours for lunch at home, they made up for it by going out for dinner as late as 10 pm. It took some getting used to, but it was all an adaptation to a hot climate.

I spent nearly the last of my budgeted funds on a gift for my _senorita_ from Madrid. Taking a complete stranger under her wing as she did, she deserved it.

I was about to catch a train for the South when two English women at my hotel offered me a ride for a share of the expenses. The scenery was harsh, bare, and monotonous--one identical village after another of white-washed houses with red-tiled roofs. Our destination, Granada, was different, lush and green. It was the home of The Alhambra, a palace from the time when the Moors ruled southern Spain. It was magical--and there were no tourists.

The overnight train ride back to Madrid was a nightmare. The rail car was crowded and stuffy. It reeked of salami, garlic, and perspiration. Folks were friendly enough; there were just too many of them. The seats were bare wood with no cushions. The train stopped every ten minutes at places that weren't even crossroads. It was torture.

I had planned to take another train to London but decided to treat myself to a flight. I made sure to get a room in London before I left Madrid.

I could have taken guided tours during my ten weeks in Europe, but I preferred the spontaneity of traveling alone. I was never lonely. I always seemed to meet someone.

7.
Bluebells and Bamboo

I was thirty-one. I eventually wanted a wife, but I first needed a girlfriend. My approach to the challenge was methodical. I lived in a Maryland suburb of Washington, DC, and subscribed to the **Post**, whose Friday edition included a detailed listing of exhibits, openings, and activities for the weekend. I read it each week, searching for ones that appealed to me, hoping they would attract a like-minded woman.

In April 1973, I found a course, "Introduction to Wildflowers," sponsored by a local trail club. On two consecutive Saturdays, in a local nature preserve, there would be a guided walk with lectures. I had been gardening since I was thirteen, and this was perfect. At the least, I could discover native species for my garden; at best, I might meet the love of my life.

On the first Saturday, a group of twenty showed up. Our guides were two elderly women. They were charming, as were the flowers, but once I noticed a certain woman in the group, I kept one eye on the violets and the other on her. There was a quiet calm about her that I found appealing, and I eased my way over to where she was gazing down at trout lilies. Four inches tall, their bright yellow trumpet flowers with recurved petals looked exactly like miniature lilies. Our guides had already lectured on them and moved on to other specimens, but her continuing interest gave me an opening:

"Do you know why they are called "trout lilies?"

"Oh, hello. Well, they're tiny, but they do look like lilies."

 "Right, but why "trout?"

"I don't know."

"You see the brown mottling and spots on their leaves? They look just like the markings on a brown trout."

"Thank you. Of all we've seen here, they are my favorite.

"Mine too."

As she spoke, she gave me a melting smile. It seemed to dissolve the boundaries that keep people apart. *Could she be the one?*

We introduced ourselves. She was Susan. From then on, we did not attempt to catch up with the group but simply ambled at our own pace.

Suddenly, the path before us turned a brilliant blue. We had come upon a host of bluebells. Up to that point, the flowers we had been seeing were small and inconspicuous, easily overlooked if the ladies had not pointed them out. These were bold and stunning.

"Susan, these beauties are my new favorites."

"Oh, I agree." Again, we were on the same wavelength. *She really might be the one.*

Along with flowers, I was infatuated with photography. Around my neck hung two 35 mm single-lens reflex cameras, and my pockets were stuffed with the lenses for them. I wore a safari jacket, the only garment I knew of that could hold all my gear. On my back was a full-frame backpack, the type used for wilderness hiking—again, the only type large enough for my cameras and accessories.

As we stood transfixed by the bluebells, I asked Susan if she would mind posing among them. I explained that a human figure helped establish the scale of objects in a photo, and she could provide the missing element. That was true, but I wanted a photo of her, not the bluebells.

She crouched low and added a touch of her own. Breaking off a few stems, she created a bouquet, which she held in a position just right for the composition. She had fulfilled a second principle of photography: a scene is more interesting if someone is doing something in it.

When we had finished filming, I thanked her for the performance. "You created a beautiful picture."

"Is that why you shot a whole roll of film?"

She said it sweetly, with one of those smiles, but I feared she had guessed my true motive in taking the photo. Perhaps I had been gazing at her legs. I hoped not, but I honestly didn't know. Something strange had happened. When she was positioning herself with the bouquet, I noticed for the first time that she had lovely, shapely legs. She was wearing shorts, which had never concealed them, but I had been oblivious. A strong sense of her presence had overshadowed the details of her appearance. That had never happened before with anyone.

Now that I was appreciating her this way, however, I did not want to lose sight of what had drawn me to her from the start: her inner beauty. This was all very strange.

Pursuing the photography theme, I suggested we meet for the walk the following week after I got the film developed so I could give her the photos. When she showed up the next Saturday, I was pleased to see my plan had worked. Later, however, she told me she had come, not for the photos, but because she had found me amusing and strangely interesting. She had never seen anyone so bizarrely dressed or photographically equipped and wanted to learn more.

After the second Saturday, we had our first date. We met at my apartment and drove to a nearby state park. There, fresh from our course, we strolled along a trail, trying to remember which wildflower was which. We did not do well, probably because we had gone our own way and missed half the lectures.

On the ride back, we stopped at a country general store for sandwiches.

When I opened my wallet to pay, it was empty. For the first time, Susan was no longer smiling. Her expression said it all: "Who is this character, and why am I with him?" She darkened further, if possible when I removed the belt from the waist of my pants. I am sure she was about to shout for help when I showed her a zipper on the belt, undid it, and withdrew a twenty-dollar bill. It was a money belt. I was absent-minded, and, as I had just demonstrated, the belt was a reasonable precaution. The relief on her face was palpable. Then she gave me another of those melting smiles: "You are a bit eccentric, aren't you?"

Fortunately, we had ordered different meals because thirty minutes later, hers made her throw up. She lowered her window in time to avoid a complete catastrophe, but she looked and felt a mess. We headed for my apartment and a change of clothes.

My first thought was to offer her my robe. It was short and would hardly have covered her hips, leaving bare those long, lovely legs. I caught myself. She needed to be cared for, not stared at. Instead, I loaned her an oversized safari shirt and a pair of long pants. She still looked appealing but in a safer, more innocent way.

Still recovering, she stayed all afternoon. As we sat quietly on my sofa, I pointed to a bowl of nuts on the coffee table before us. "You see those nuts? I swear they have been disappearing lately."

"Are you a nibbler?"

"Not of nuts, no. And no one has been here."

Cupping an ear with a hand, she said, "I hear something in that wall."

She was right. I could hear it, too. It was coming from behind a square-foot metal door that provided access to pipes behind the wall. Whoever had been tinkering there last had failed to latch the door shut, and it was ajar a couple of inches. We could hear the rustling more clearly now, and I gingerly opened the door to peek. We discovered three piles of nuts, sorted by type: filberts, walnuts, and pecans. Cowering in the shadows behind them, frozen with fear, was a squirrel.

With all the gravity I could simulate, I told her I had trained the animal to collect and organize the nuts to entertain my girlfriends.

"Does that mean I am your girlfriend?"

"If you want to be."

"I might."

It was only playful banter, but she might be feeling some stirrings for me, too. I hoped so.

Susan was still feeling weak and decided to stay the night. It was getting late, and I suggested we continue chatting in bed and try to get some sleep. We lay there fully clothed. We might have been more comfortable in pajamas, but she needed rest, and I needed no further distractions. I never said a word.

We were both dozing off when suddenly a bird burst into full-throated song. It was ten p.m. We had never heard a bird sing at night, but this one was proceeding at full throttle. It was near.

I had a ground-floor apartment. We looked out the bedroom window, where a mulberry tree stood only inches away. On the highest branch was a mockingbird, singing so hard its breast was heaving. Mimicking one melodious birdsong after another, it was stringing them together like multi-colored gems on a necklace. The creature sang without pause until dawn when all the other birds joined in at their regular time. Their calls seemed pitiably bland in comparison.

The next morning, Susan remembered only a little of our singing bird. She had fallen asleep after thirty minutes. I had not slept at all but lay awake enthralled. To me, the mockingbird was a sign: *Yes, she was the one.*

She soon reached a similar conclusion and gave up her apartment. Mine was larger and had a garden, albeit larcenous in origin. Without asking permission from the landlord, I had brazenly carved it from the landscaped lawn around my patio. I started small, but after several years there, I had dug up ten feet of their boring turf to create a flowerbed. Susan was surprised when I confessed my trespasses but soon benefitted from them as she joined me in cultivating what I had planted there. We continued our criminal horticulture for a year before new, less tolerant management shut us down. We escaped eviction but had to dig up our gorgeous peonies and dahlias and restore the turf.

We could not continue living without plants. We got married and bought our own home. In line with our priorities, we found a property with a small house on a large lot. We were gardeners, not interior decorators. As it happened, our backyard directly joined a wild, sprawling regional park. The property line lay buried somewhere between the two beneath robust stands of bamboo that thrived there.

At first, we welcomed the bamboo as an exotic addition to our domestic plants; it began moving our way and spreading throughout the yard. From a network of underground runners, shoots appeared overnight. We not only tripped over them; we ran the risk of being impaled since they emerged from the ground as foot-long sharp-pointed spears.

We attacked the intruder with an axe and chainsaw but could not control it. Bamboo grew a foot a day and was soon our main crop. We did take the precaution of spray-painting new spears bright orange to avoid grievous harm, but the backyard was a total loss. We managed to confine the stalks to the back and grew more reasonable plants in the front, but we had learned the hard way: plants have personalities.

Some, like bamboo, are bullies who will crowd out everything else. Others, like our beloved trout lilies and bluebells, are gentle souls who bloom reliably in harmony with others.

My Susan was a wildflower, and my instincts had been right: she definitely was *the one.* She was my bluebell.